GLOSSARY

Allah	Arabic word for GOD.
Adhan	Call for prayer.
Dua	Asking Allah for blessings upon yourself and others.
Iftar	Evening meal.
Insha-Allah	If Allah wills.
Quran	The holy book of Islam.
Masjid	Arabic word for mosque.
Mubarak	Blessed.
Salat	The prayer of Muslims performed five times a day.
Suhoor	The meal before dawn.

In the middle of the night, Laila hears a sound coming from the kitchen.

Rubbing her eyes, she gets out of bed and goes downstairs to see what is happening.

Laila finds her family seated at the dining table, having a meal.

"A meal at this time?" Laila wonders.

Tell me MORE about Ramadan

Bachar Karroum

ILLUSTRATOR - TANJA VARCELIJA

ISBN: 978-1-988779-01-0

Dépôt légal : bibliothèque et archives nationales du Québec, 2018.
Dépôt légal : bibliothèque et archives Canada, 2018.

Author   : **Bachar Karroum**
Illustrator   : **Tanja Varcelija**
Graphic Designer : **Samuel Gabriel**
Editor   : **Christina Cutting**

The sun is up, and so is Laila.

"Mom! I'm hungry!" yells Laila.

"Breakfast is on the table!" Mom replies.

Laila runs downstairs, sits at the table, and waits for her family.

"Nobody's having breakfast?" Laila is surprised.

In the evening, Laila is pleased to see the whole family at home.

Her grandparents, aunt, uncle and cousins, almost everyone is there.

Laila is very happy! She loves being surrounded by family.

"But what could be the occasion?" Laila asks herself.

As the sun goes down, the kitchen gets crowded.

Everyone is giving a hand, preparing the meal, and setting the table.

Collaboration and family spirit are at their most.

Laila would love this great atmosphere every day.

The table is ready and everyone is seated. However, no one is eating.
The whole family is waiting.

Suddenly, Laila hears the Adhan being called out from the Masjid nearby.

After breaking the fast and saying the Iftar's Dua, everyone begins to eat,
in silence.

Laila observes everything without making a sound.

When the meal is over, some go to the Masjid to pray and others pray at home.

The atmosphere is peaceful and comforting.

Laila is very happy, yet she really wants to know what the occasion is.

Later that night, Laila goes to see her father.

"Dad, is today a special day?" Laila questions.

"Oh Laila! It's the first day of the holy month of Ramadan.
I'm sorry we didn't tell you.

Now since you're a big girl, let me tell you more," says Dad.

"During this month, we don't eat or drink from dawn to sunset," Dad explains.

Laila remembers what she saw earlier that day.

"So that's why I saw you have a meal in the middle of the night!" shouts Laila.

"Yes, that's right! It's the Suhoor, the meal before dawn. Clever girl!"

"But you know, Laila, Ramadan is not just about staying away from food and drink, it's..."

"...a month of mercy where the doors of paradise are open, so we increase prayers (Salat) and the recitation of the Quran.

Do you know the Quran was sent down during Ramadan?" Dad asks Laila.

"That's interesting. I didn't know that, Dad!" says Laila.

"Dad, tell me more about Ramadan!" requests Laila.

"Ramadan is also a month for good deeds. A month that reminds and teaches us to be forgiving, loving, caring, and generous."

"I understand. So, we are trained to be good during Ramadan, so that we can continue to be good every day!" Laila adds.

"That's right Laila," Dad agrees and continues.

"During this month, we give charity as well.

We help the needy and provide them with good food and many other things that they may need.

When you give to those in need, you'll be rewarded by Allah."

"Dad can I give some of my toys to the children in need?" asks Laila.

"That's a great idea, Laila. I'm very proud of you!" says Dad.

"Dad...I still don't understand. Why do we not eat and drink during Ramadan?"

"When we don't eat and drink, we understand what it is like to be hungry.

So, we must always be thankful to Allah for what He has given us, not waste food, and remember those who don't have much to eat."

"Ramadan is super cool! Dad, can I fast too?" Laila asks.

"Yes. You can try tomorrow. I'll wake you up for the meal before dawn Insha-Allah. Now, you better get to sleep early," Dad advises.

"Yes, I will. Ramadan Mubarak, Dad," says Laila very excited.

"Ramadan Mubarak, sweetheart."

We hope you and your children enjoyed the story!

OTHER CHILDREN'S BOOKS TO CONSIDER

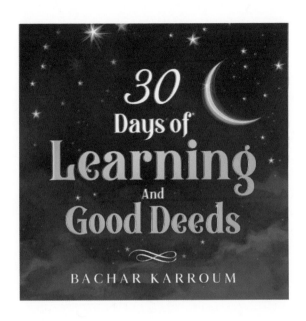

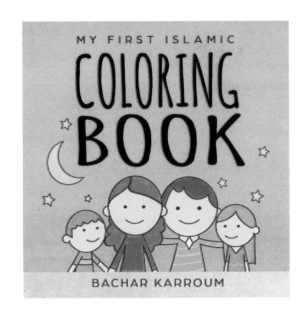

Printed in Great Britain
by Amazon

19980020R00018